MUSICAL
INSTRUMENTS
OF THE WORLD

Modern
Instruments

Barrie Carson Turner
Illustrated by John See

❧ Belitha Press

First published in the UK in 2000 by
Belitha Press Limited
London House, Great Eastern Wharf,
Parkgate Road, London SW11 4NQ

Editor: Russell McLean
Designer: Zoe Quayle
Picture researcher: Juliet Duff
Educational consultant: Celia Pardaens

ISBN 1 84138 117 9

Printed in Singapore

British Library Cataloguing in Publication Data
for this book is available from the British Library.

10 9 8 7 6 5 4 3 2 1

Picture acknowledgements:
J. Allan Cash: 12. Arena Images: 13. The Lebrecht Collection:
8 Chris Stock; 26 M. Peric; 11 Wladimir Polak; 27 Graham Salter.
Panos Pictures: 16. Performing Arts Library: 19 bottom Clive Barda;
22 Fritz Curzon; 7, 21 Steve Gillett. Redferns: 4-5, 23, 29 Mick
Hutson; 9 Leon Morris; 25 Odile Noel; 15, 17 David Redfern.
Tony Stone Images: 19 top Oliver Benn.

Contents

Musical

Musical instruments are played in every country of the world. There are many thousands of different instruments of all shapes and sizes. They are often divided into four groups: strings, brass, percussion and woodwind.

Percussion instruments are struck (hit), shaken or scraped to make their sound. Woodwind and brass instruments are blown to make their sound. String instruments make a sound when their strings vibrate.

instruments

This book is about modern instruments. Some of them are traditional instruments that have been improved or redesigned over the last 100 years using new materials. Others use modern electronics to produce their sound. Some instruments, such as the wind synthesizer and the electronic drum kit, are able to copy the exact sound of traditional instruments.

You can read about 17 instruments in this book. There is a picture of each instrument and a photograph of a performer playing it. On pages 30 and 31 you will find a list of useful words to help you understand more about music.

Electric guitar

The electric guitar has been played in rock and pop music for almost 50 years. The instrument has six steel strings and a solid body made of wood or plastic. Thin bands of metal called frets are stretched across the fingerboard. They show guitarists where to put their fingers.

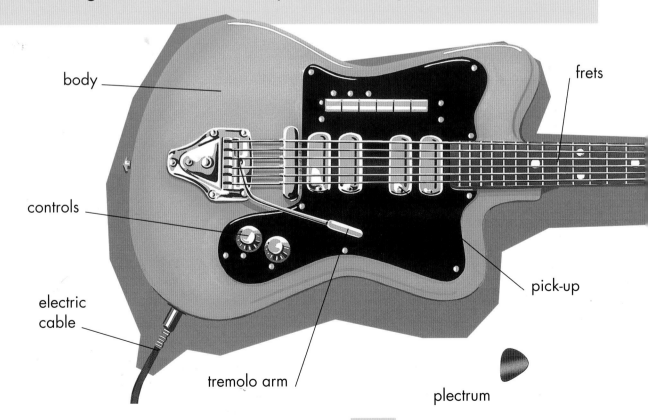

body

frets

controls

pick-up

electric cable

tremolo arm

plectrum

6

Players pluck the strings with their fingers or with a thin piece of plastic called a plectrum. The vibrations from the strings pass through a part of the guitar called a pick-up. Then they are made louder by an amplifier. The sound is heard from speakers. The player uses the controls and the tremolo arm to vary the sound of the guitar.

tuning pegs

The electric guitar is quite easy to play alongside a singer or another instrument. Many guitarists play and sing at the same time.

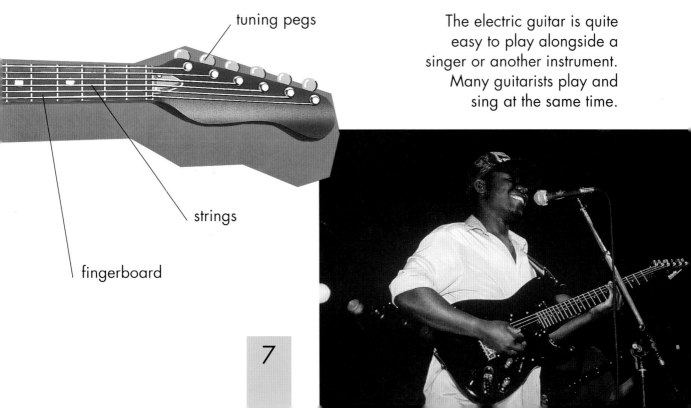

strings

fingerboard

7

Kazoo

Kazoo players hum into this instrument. A thin tissue of strong paper is stretched across a hole in the tube of the kazoo. This is called a membrane. The paper vibrates when the kazoo is blown. This changes the player's humming into a buzzing sound.

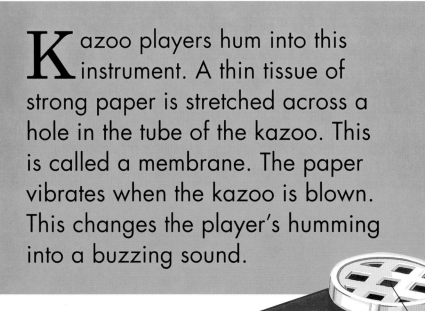

plastic tube

playing end

paper membrane beneath plastic covering

Kazoos can be made of metal or plastic. They make a strong, reedy sound.

8

Cabasa

The first cabasas were made from pear-shaped fruits called gourds. Modern instruments are often made of metal and wood. Players hold the cabasa in their right hand and twist the metal beads with their left hand. Underneath the beads are metal ridges. The beads rub against the metal to make a scraping sound.

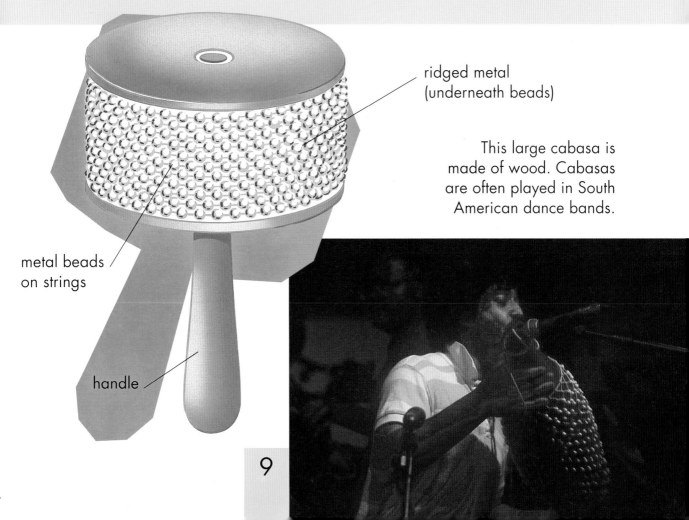

ridged metal
(underneath beads)

metal beads
on strings

handle

This large cabasa is made of wood. Cabasas are often played in South American dance bands.

Vibraphone

The metal bars of a vibraphone are laid out like a piano keyboard. Underneath each bar is a metal tube called a resonator. The resonators make the sound of the instrument louder and richer.

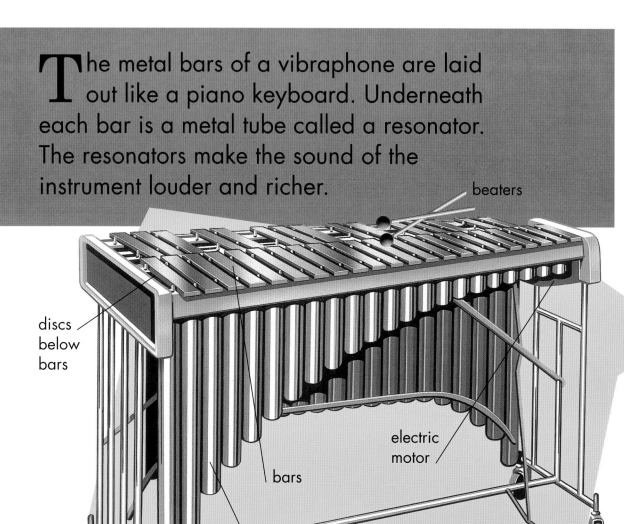

beaters

discs below bars

bars

electric motor

resonators

The vibraphone is played with soft felt beaters to make a rich, warm sound. Musicians often call the vibraphone the vibes.

Above each resonator is a round metal disc. The discs spin round when the vibraphone's electric motor is switched on. The spinning discs open and close the tops of the resonators many times every second. This adds a beautiful wavering effect to the sound of the instrument.

Hi-hat cymbal

The hi-hat cymbal is actually two cymbals. They are held one above the other on a stand, almost touching. The hi-hat is worked by a foot pedal. Pressing the pedal clashes the top cymbal against the lower one. When the player releases the pedal, a spring returns the top cymbal to its original position.

The hi-hat is one of the most important instruments in a drum kit. It makes a short, crisp sound.

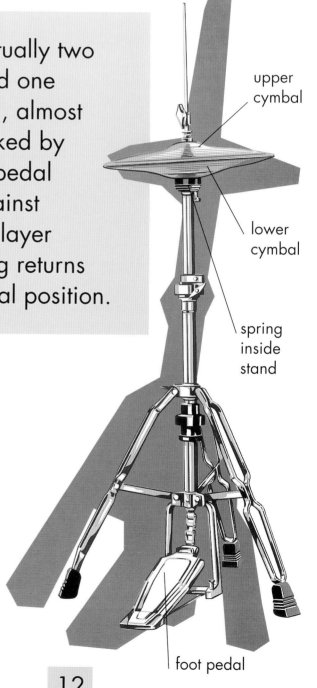

upper cymbal

lower cymbal

spring inside stand

foot pedal

12

Theremin

antenna

loop

The theremin is a very unusual instrument. It is played without the performer touching it. Around the metal antenna is a magnetic field. The player moves one hand backwards and forwards in front of the antenna. The theremin sounds when the hand enters the magnetic field. The other hand moves over a metal loop which makes the sounds loud or soft.

wooden case

The theremin makes a wailing sound like a siren. The sounds are heard through a speaker. This musician is playing a home-made theremin.

Hammond organ

The Hammond organ is different from a church organ because it has no pipes. The sound is made electronically. Above the keyboards is a row of sliding switches. These are called drawbars. They change the sound of the note being played, in the same way as the stops on a church organ.

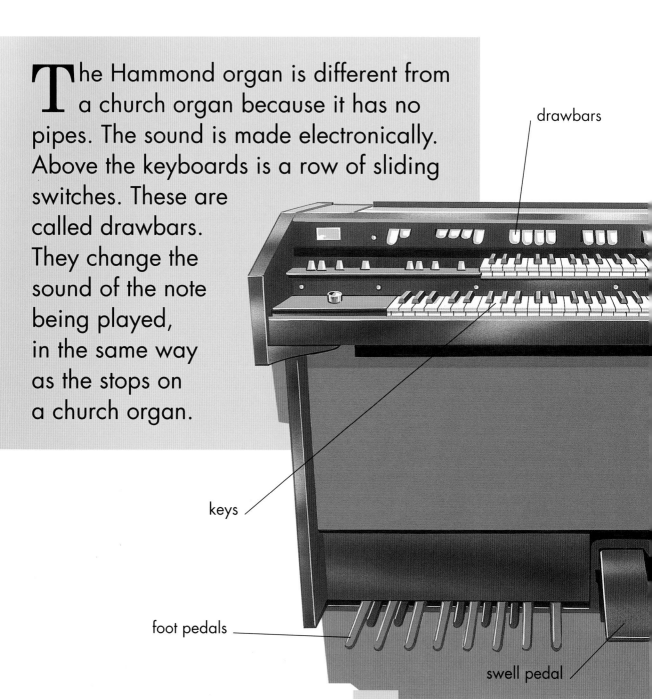

drawbars

keys

foot pedals

swell pedal

14

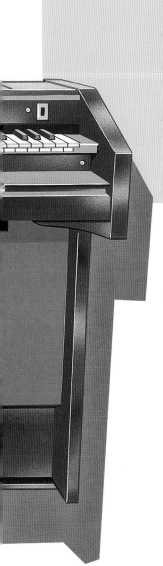

At the bottom of the instrument is a row of pedals. They are laid out like a keyboard. They are played by the feet and produce the organ's lowest sounds. A swell pedal makes the sound of the organ suddenly swell louder. Hammond organs were once very popular in homes and churches.

The Hammond organ was first played in 1935. It usually has two keyboards, called manuals.

15

Agogo bells

Agogo bells were originally played in Africa, and then South America. Modern bells are a popular percussion instrument in Latin American bands. Each instrument has two bells. They are shaped like long cones, and are joined together by a curved metal handle. Each bell sounds a different note.

large bell sounds low notes

beater

small bell sounds high notes

Agogo bells have no clappers. They are struck with a metal rod to make a bright, clear sound.

Hawaiian guitar

The Hawaiian guitar is an electric guitar which sits on the player's knees, or rests on a stand. Thin metal bands called frets show the position of the notes on the fingerboard. Players slide a steel bar from note to note. This gives the instrument its other name of slide guitar. The Hawaiian guitar was first played on the island of Hawaii.

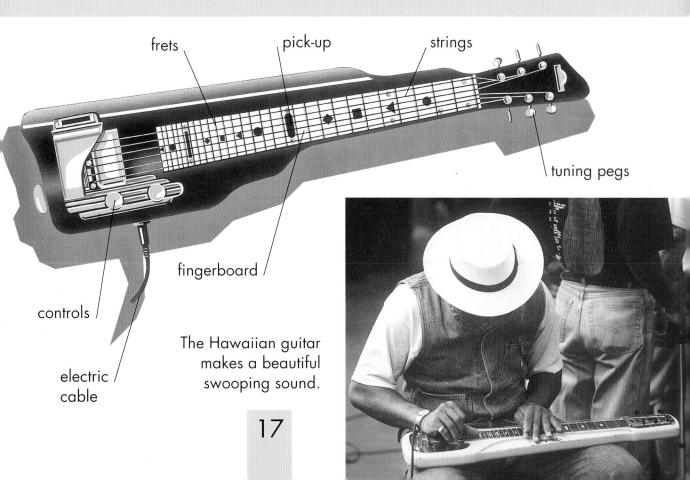

frets

pick-up

strings

tuning pegs

fingerboard

controls

electric cable

The Hawaiian guitar makes a beautiful swooping sound.

17

Marimba

The marimba is like a giant xylophone. It makes a rich, deep sound. The wooden bars are laid out like a keyboard. Under each bar, or note, is a metal tube called a resonator. The resonators make the sound richer and more mellow.

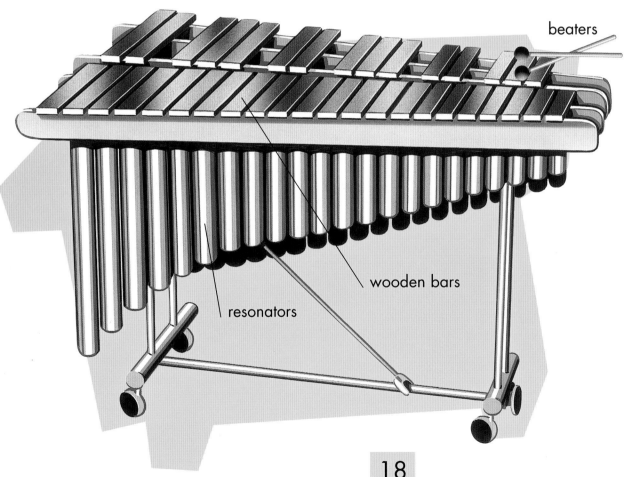

beaters

wooden bars

resonators

Some marimbas are large enough to be played by several musicians at once.

Marimba players often hold two beaters in each hand. This allows them to play up to four notes at a time.

Heavy beaters are needed to produce a good sound from the marimba. The beaters have soft heads to avoid damaging the bars. Early marimbas had resonators made from gourds (a fruit shaped like a pear). They made a higher sound than modern orchestral marimbas.

19

Bass guitar

The electric bass guitar has a solid body made of wood or plastic. It has four metal strings. They are thick and heavy. The bass guitar is held around the player's neck by a strap. Across the fingerboard are thin strips of metal called frets. They show players where to put their fingers.

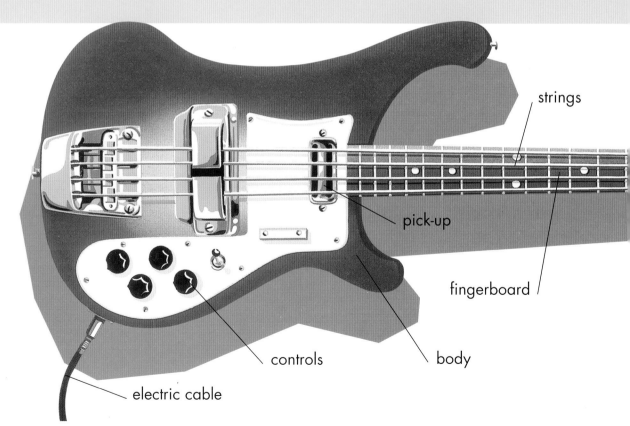

strings

pick-up

fingerboard

controls

body

electric cable

The sound of the bass guitar is very low. Players usually pluck the strings with their fingers. When a string is plucked, the vibrations travel through the pick-ups to the amplifier, and then to the speakers. The player uses the controls to vary the sound of the bass guitar.

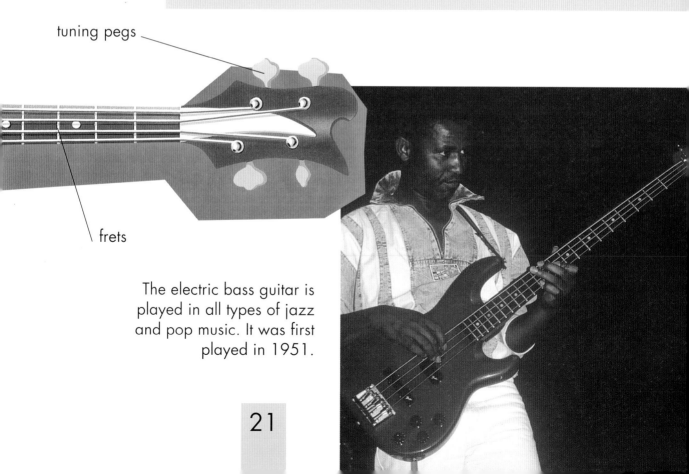

tuning pegs

frets

The electric bass guitar is played in all types of jazz and pop music. It was first played in 1951.

21

Electric violin

The electric violin is played in exactly the same way as a normal violin. The vibrations made by the strings pass through a pick-up. The sounds are made louder by an amplifier, and then heard from speakers. Controls allow the player to vary the sound of the violin. The electric violin has a slender, flat body.

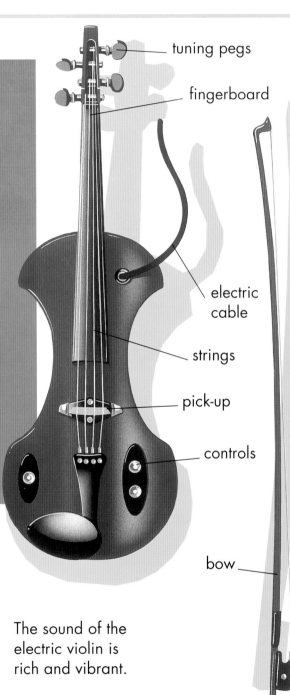

tuning pegs

fingerboard

electric cable

strings

pick-up

controls

bow

The sound of the electric violin is rich and vibrant.

Electronic drums

Electronic drum kits have round pads of rubber or plastic rather than drums and cymbals. When the drummer strikes the pads, electronic sounds are heard through speakers. The pads allow the drum sticks to bounce slightly – just as they would if they were striking a real drum skin.

drum and cymbal pads

An electronic drum kit can play many more sounds than a standard drum kit.

controls

drum sticks

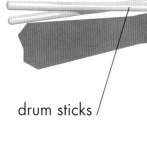

23

Ondes martenot

The ondes martenot (ond-mar-tin-o) was invented by a French musician, Maurice Martenot. It has a small keyboard connected to speakers. The instrument can only play one note at a time. When a key is pressed, the sound is created electronically and then amplified through the speakers. Inside a small drawer are controls. They create loud or soft notes, as well as special sounds.

music stand

control drawer

keyboard

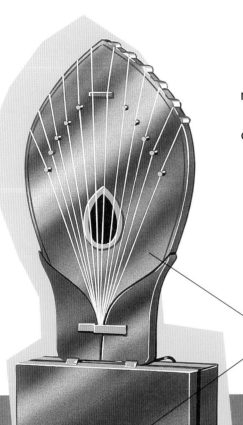

Ondes martenot players wear a metal ring on their right hand. It works a control which allows the sound of each note to slide into the next.

speakers

The French word *ondes* means waves. The inventor used this word to describe the smooth rising and falling sound of the instrument. The ondes martenot can be heard in many film soundtracks.

Metal guiro

Guiro (jy-roe) is another name for scraper. Scrapers have a pattern of ridges cut into them. The player scrapes a metal rod across the ridges to make a rasping, scratching sound. Early guiros were made from bark, or from a fruit called a gourd. The modern metal guiro is played in South American dance bands. It marks the beat of the music.

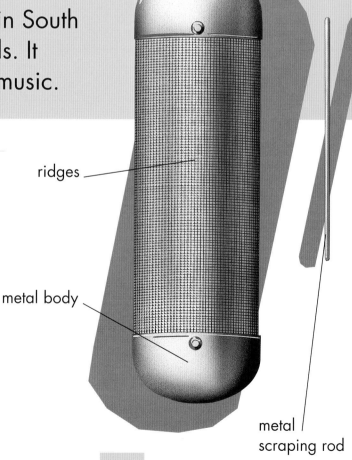

ridges

metal body

metal scraping rod

This metal guiro is tube shaped. The musician is using it to accompany his singing.

Wind synthesizer

The wind synthesizer is an electronic woodwind instrument. It is played in the same way as an ordinary instrument. When the player presses the keys, electronic signals travel to a control box. Here the signals are turned into the sound the player wants. From the control box the sounds travel to the speakers.

mouthpiece

keys

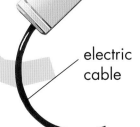

electric cable

Electronic wind instruments can make many more sounds than an ordinary wind instrument.

Electric piano

The electric piano became popular with jazz and pop musicians in the 1960s. Although the instrument has strings and hammers, it works differently from an ordinary piano.

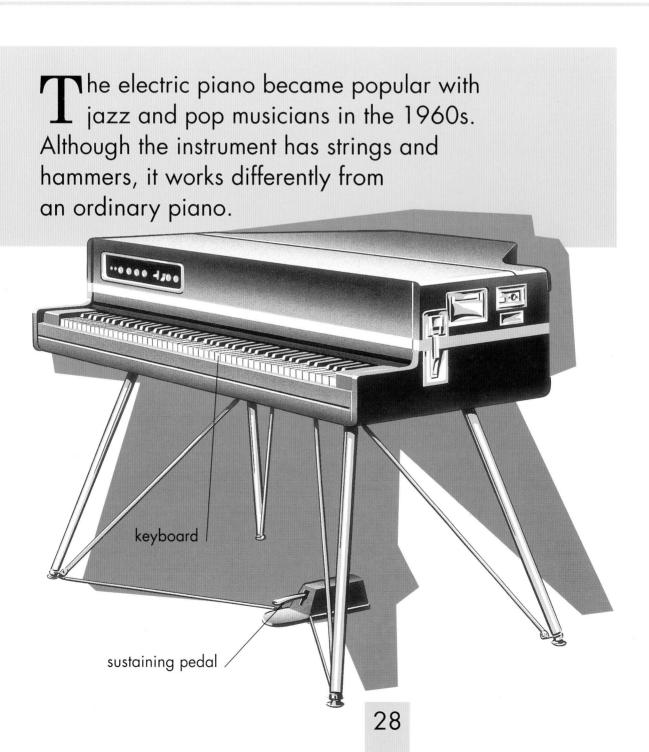

keyboard

sustaining pedal

There is one short string, called a tine, for each note. When a key is pressed, a small hammer hits the tine. The tine makes a very quiet sound. This is made louder by an amplifier, and then heard through speakers. The instrument can play loud and soft notes, just like an ordinary piano.

The electric piano has a lever called a sustaining pedal. Players press the pedal with their right foot. This allows the sound to continue after the player has lifted their hands from the keyboard.

The electric piano became popular with pop and jazz bands because it is easy to pack away and carry.

29

Words to

accompaniment Notes that are played along with a tune.

accompany To play music alongside a singer or another player who has the tune.

amplifier A machine which makes the sound of an instrument louder.

beat The steady pulse of the music.

beaters Sticks of wood or wire used to strike some instruments. The ends may be made of felt or rubber.

chords Groups of notes played together.

clapper A small piece of metal inside a bell. The clapper strikes the sides of the bell to make it sound.

drawbars Switches on a Hammond organ which change the sound of each keyboard.

fingerboard A long strip of wood or plastic glued to the neck of a string instrument. The player presses the strings against the fingerboard to make the different notes.

frets Thin strips, usually made of metal, on a fingerboard. They show players where to put their fingers to make the notes on an instrument.

manual An organ keyboard.

melody A tune.

membrane A thin sheet of strong paper or other material.

pedal Any part of an instrument worked by the player's foot.

pick-up The part of a string instrument that picks up the vibrations of the strings.

30

remember

plectrum A small piece of plastic or other material, used to pluck some string instruments.

pluck To play an instrument by pulling the strings quickly with the fingers, and letting go again.

resonators Metal tubes beneath the bars of a marimba or a vibraphone. They make the sound of the instrument louder and more rounded.

rhythm A rhythm is made by the beat of the music, and by how long and short the notes are.

soundtrack The music which accompanies a film.

speakers The sounds of electric and electronic instruments are heard through speakers. The word speakers is short for loudspeakers.

strike To play an instrument by hitting it.

sustaining pedal A lever operated by the foot which allows the notes of a keyboard instrument to sound for longer.

swell pedal A pedal on an electronic organ or piano that makes the music suddenly sound louder.

tines The short strings on an electric piano.

tuning pegs Pegs that are turned to tighten or loosen the strings of an instrument until they sound the right note.

vibrations The fast shaking of an object, such as a string. Strings vibrate when they are plucked.

31

Index

agogo bells 16
amplifier 7, 21, 22, 24, 29, 30

bands 9, 16, 26, 29
bars 10, 18, 19
bass guitar 20-21
beaters 10, 11, 16, 18, 19, 30

cabasa 9
clapper 16, 30
controls 6, 7, 17, 20, 21, 22, 23, 24, 27

dance music 9, 26
drawbars 14, 30

electric guitar 6-7, 17
electric piano 28-29
electric violin 22
electronic drums 5, 23

fingerboard 6, 7, 17, 20, 22, 30
frets 6, 17, 20, 21, 30

gourds 9, 19, 26

hammer 28, 29
Hammond organ 14-15
Hawaiian guitar 17
hi-hat cymbal 12

jazz 21, 28, 29

kazoo 8
keyboard 10, 14, 15, 18, 24, 28, 29

magnetic field 13
manual 15, 30
marimba 18-19
membrane 8, 30
metal guiro 26

ondes martenot 24-25
orchestra 19

pedal 12, 14, 15, 30
percussion instruments 4, 16
piano 10, 28, 29
pick-up 6, 7, 17, 20, 21, 22, 30
plectrum 6, 7, 31
pop music 6, 21, 28

resonator 10, 11, 18, 19, 31
rock music 6

soundtrack 25, 31
speakers 7, 13, 21, 22, 23, 24, 27, 29, 31
strings 4, 6, 7, 17, 20, 21, 22, 28, 29
sustaining pedal 28, 29, 31
swell pedal 14, 15, 31

theremin 13
tine 29, 31
tremolo arm 6, 7
tuning pegs 7, 17, 21, 22, 31

vibraphone 10-11
vibrations 4, 7, 8, 21, 22, 31

wind synthesizer 5, 27
woodwind instruments 4, 27